A FAN'S GUIDE TO NFL FREE AGENCY HITS AND MISSES

CASE STUDIES AND LESSONS LEARNED FROM LANDMARK SIGNINGS THROUGHOUT HISTORY

BRUCE IRONS

WOLF MOUNTAIN
- PUBLISHING -

ISBN 978-1-952286-03-2 (paperback)

ISBN 978-1-952286-02-5 (ebook)

"You had better do your homework... it's not fantasy football."

- Bill Polian, former General Manager of the Buffalo Bills, Carolina Panthers, and Indianapolis Colts, and 6-time NFL Executive of the Year, discussing NFL free agency

CONTENTS

DEDICATION

Dedicated to the men who risk their lives and physical well-being so we can be entertained on Sundays, and to Andy, Mike, and Dustin for talking to me about it too much.

INTRODUCTION

Do you like football? Do you like watching your team every Sunday in the fall? Do you want a deeper understanding of how your team was built? Do you want to appreciate the game a little more?

Then this book is for you!

In this guide, we'll look back at some of the biggest hits and misses in the history of NFL free agency to find key lessons that teams and fans can learn.

We'll also get a full understanding of how the salary cap, player contracts, and bonuses work and the role they play in free agency and in creating a winning team.

Big-name stars becoming free agents and signing mega-deals is one of the most exciting parts of every NFL offseason. Soon after the euphoria of the Super Bowl wears off, free agency excitement begins.

But what happens when the dust settles?

Where does all the excitement around the celebrated signings go?

Why does it seem to fade away by the time the following season starts to wind down?

Why do we rarely talk about all the big name free agent signings when the new champion hoists the Lombardi trophy?

Free agency - the chance to add a proven, top-flight star to a team - is an enticing deal, but history shows us that the biggest contracts for the biggest free agent targets (like Mario Williams's six year, $100M deal with the Bills in 2012, Ndamukong Suh's 6 year, $114M deal with the Dolphins in 2015, or Kirk Cousins's blockbuster, fully guaranteed, three year, $84M deal with the Vikings in 2018), usually don't end with a championship.

Building a football team is a complex job because football is a more complex sport than its peers.

Baseball is a game of pitcher versus batter and defender versus ball. If you're the batter, you're waiting to hit the ball. If you're in the field, you're waiting to see where the ball is hit. Baseball is so analytical because the environment is so controlled.

Basketball features a small number of two-way players and is a game of one-on-one matchups. If you're on offense, you're either going to shoot, or pass to one of your four teammates. If you're on defense, you have one man or one area to guard. It's a confined game.

Football is different. It's not controlled and it's not confined.

In football, twenty-two players with specialized roles are all running in different directions in loosely orchestrated chaos. If any one of those players blows their assignment one time, the play - or even the game - can be lost.

In baseball and basketball, the best collection of players usually wins. In football, the best *team* wins - the whole can (and should) be much greater than the sum of the parts.

This makes building a team, and handling free agency, all the more difficult.

In this book, we'll look back at some of the toughest free agent situations teams have found themselves in to look for the lessons history provides.

But before we get into the case studies and lessons, we need to understand the context that free agency works in.

The National Football League is not 32 individual teams just running their own independent businesses. There's a lot of legal stuff behind the scenes, but the simplest way to think about it is that the NFL is one business and the 32 teams are each like network offices of that business.

The NFL players are all a part of one big union, and they negotiated a Collective Bargaining Agreement (CBA) with the owners (and a whole bunch of accountants) to establish some reasonable ground rules for doing business together. The salary cap, player tags, and how contracts handled are all covered in the CBA.

The CBA gives us all we need to know to understand free agency, so we'll start there.

PART I

FREE AGENCY, SALARY CAP, AND PLAYER CONTRACTS

FREE AGENCY

Building an NFL team is hard.

Most players join their first team through the draft, but draft picks are never guaranteed to work out. As a result, teams always have holes to fill.

That's where free agency comes in!

A marvelous cure-all for the roster problems of every team... or so they hope.

Free agency is a simple concept: players sign contracts with teams to play for a certain period of time (usually around 4 years) and when that contract is up, the player is free to sign with whichever team they like.

This is great for players - it allows a reasonable level of freedom and mobility, while also creating a free market where they can maximize their earnings.

It's great for teams, too - their rivals can't just hog good players forever and if a team wants a star player, all they have to do is pay for them.

That's where things get interesting.

Let's say you're the General Manager and you want to sign a free agent.

Every time you sign a player in free agency, you're winning a bidding war against 31 other teams - you're paying more than the team that has been watching him practice and gameplan and play for the last four years.

Ever buy a used car and think "Wow, this thing runs great - why on Earth would they be selling this?"

Well, imagine a purchase like that, but you're spending $100M dollars, and everyone else with an opportunity to buy that car, unanimously agrees it isn't worth the price and laughs at you behind your back. Then thousands of fans from the other 31 teams take to Twitter to call you a moron for buying that car.

Oh, and if the car breaks down, you lose your job (which is an awesome job because you get paid a ton of money for watching and talking about football all day). Oh, and people who get fired from that particular job usually don't ever get a chance to do that job again.

Those big moves can be stressful.

Free agency is not for the faint of heart.

It's hard to judge football players and place a value on their skills. Sure, you can watch how they played for another team, but you don't know how they'll fit in your scheme, you don't know if they'll cause problems in your locker room, and you don't know if they'll stop trying so hard once they get a big contract in free agency.

You also don't know how the player will respond to the simple passage of time. These are human beings who beat up their bodies for our entertainment - they wear down.

The average length of an NFL career is around 3.3

years. That stat is a little misleading, though, because that average is lowered considerably by fringe players who don't last very long. The guys with the skills to really make it in this league last a little longer.

Most skill position players (running back, wide receiver, defensive back) start to notice a drop-off around age 30 as the years catch up. Linemen can usually last a few more years and the fancy, protected players like kickers, punters, and quarterbacks last the longest, but they all wear down eventually. One of the problems with free agency is understanding when.

All these factors play into the choices on free agents (including the ones that are already on your own team). Once all those options have been weighted, teams have to take action, which means diving into the accounting of player contracts and the salary cap.

2

UNDERSTANDING THE SALARY CAP

S hortly after the advent of free agency in 1993, the league realized it needed a salary cap. If free agency were implemented without a salary cap, teams with the most money (i.e., those in the biggest cities and with the richest owners) could attempt to buy a title by out-bidding other teams for all the best players.

This is what sets the NFL salary cap apart from other leagues: the NFL salary cap exists, in large part, to create a degree of parity. Parity leads to more competitive games, which makes for a more entertaining league. This is why any team can beat any other team on any given Sunday.

The salary cap rules in the NFL are far more strict than those of the NBA or MLB. Sure, teams in the NFL can defer some money forward, and there are ways to distribute cap hits, but the piper always has to be paid. The rules are a lot more flexible in other sports.

Major League Baseball doesn't have a salary cap. Prior to the start of the 2020 MLB season, the New York Yankees had a payroll of over $240M, while the Miami Marlins were under $45M. The luxury tax model allows teams to simply outspend other teams in an effort to buy a title.

The NBA has a "salary cap" of sorts, but also uses a luxury tax model like MLB, along with a host of other exceptions that focus more on capping what owners have to spend than creating competitive balance. With only five players from a team on the court at a time, players often use free agency as an opportunity to form super-teams, a trend that started when back-to-back MVP LeBron James and four-time All-Star Chris Bosh both decided to join six-time All-Star Dwyane Wade on the Miami Heat in 2010.

In the NFL, there are 22 players on the field at a time and each game is impacted by over 100 players and dozens of coaches. With that many players, it's impossible to make a super team like in the NBA. And with stricter cap rules than MLB, NFL teams simply cannot attempt to buy a championship like they can in baseball.

Building a winning team in the NFL is far more challenging than that.

The salary cap is a hard cap, but it's also a bit of a fluid accounting construct.

Let's say the salary cap is $100M. That means each team gets $100M to spend on players for that season (coaches, executives, and other employees do not count towards the cap).

If a team only spends $90M one year, they can roll over $10M of cap credit and add it to their "adjusted" cap for the following season. This means that the team would be able to spend $110M the following year, even if the salary cap were to remain the same at $100M.

A team could not, however, spend more than the cap one year and then take a cap penalty the following year.

The salary cap number changes from year to year, too. So if the cap was $100M one year, and $105M the following year, and a team were to only spend $90M one year, they would have an adjusted cap of $115M the following year.

The changes in the cap each year are based on a percentage of total revenue for the league, which means it could go up or down (though it has never gone down... yet).

When the players signed the CBA, they wanted to make sure they got their fair share of that revenue, so there is a stipulation that teams are required to spend at least 89% of their cap within four year windows. This means they could underspend in some years and make up for it in others as long as, at the end of the four-year window, they've spent 89% of their cumulative cap numbers.

So there you have it: a percentage of league revenues determines the cap each year, teams can roll unused dollars forward, and you have to pay all your players from it.

Next, we have to figure out how to pay the players.

3
_____

HOW PLAYER CONTRACTS WORK

P layer contracts, like most contracts, aren't as easy as they seem.

In most jobs, people get a salary or a wage and (if they're lucky) a bonus at the end of the year.

Player contracts in the NFL are similar, but there are a lot of little details to work through.

Teams use lots of tools in player contracts to manage a team budget under a salary cap. The major categories of compensation are:

- Base Salary
- Signing Bonus
- Other Bonuses and Incentives

Each one of them has a different purpose and different ways of accounting within the salary cap. To add another layer of complexity, NFL contracts are not guaranteed.

Teams can rip up a contract at any point and cut a player without paying them anything else in the future (which is why holdouts are so prevalent).

BASE SALARY

The foundation of most contracts is the base salary. This is the amount that teams pay a player each year.

When players come into the league, they get a predefined contract based on what slot they were drafted in. When that first contract is up, players are eligible for free agency and things start to get interesting.

After that pre-defined rookie deal is up, and the player becomes a free agent, what should his salary be?

It usually ends up being whatever the highest-bidding team offers.

Let's look at the hypothetical contract for the hypothetical player Bruce Irons, Jr. (fingers crossed).

Let's say Bruce Junior just finished his rookie deal, and some team offers him a new five-year contract for $10M.

Sounds like a nice number, but not all five-year $10M contracts are created equally. The structure matters. A lot.

It would be simple to spread the total compensation out evenly and pay out $2M each year.

But things are rarely simple when we're talking about the salary cap, and player contracts.

What if a team isn't sure about how good a player will be? They might want to have some cheap years up front to see if the player is really worth it. Maybe they only want to pay $1M each of the first two years and then $2.33M for each of the final three years.

Teams often spread the base salary of a pay out in uneven increments.

Teams may push larger payments into the future because they expect the cap to increase in the future. Maybe they pay out $3M in the first year, then $1M for the next three years, and finally $4M in the final year.

Teams may pay larger amounts in earlier years if they have available cap space and think they'll need extra money in future years to sign other players. That $10M contract could pay out $3M in each of the first two years and then $1M in each of the last three years if their quarterback's contract will be expiring in two years and they think they will need to have extra cap space available to re-sign him.

The key feature of base salary is that it only counts against the cap if it is paid, and it's only paid if the player is still on the team.

So if Bruce Junior has a deal for $2M per year for five years and he gets cut after two years, then the next three years of base salary isn't paid and they have freed up cap space. If he signs a deal that pays $1M in each of the first four years with a big balloon payment of $6M in the fifth year, he won't see most of the contract value paid out unless he plays all five years.

This means that players tend to want more of larger salaries up front (to make sure they get paid before the later years when the risk of being cut goes up) and teams (in addition to the other balancing factors discussed) tend to want larger salaries at the end of a contract term (so they have the flexibility to cut the player and save the money if they aren't performing).

One final note on base salary: base salary for each year is paid out in 17 equal weekly installments over the course of the regular season. So if a player is cut mid-season, his checks stop coming in (and the cap isn't charged).

SIGNING BONUS

Signing bonus is one of the most common ways teams and players can flex compensation to manage the cap. It's also one of the most complex accounting procedures. Pretty much every contact (with the exception of undrafted free agents) includes some level of signing bonus.

Let's say Star Receiver gets a four-year $40M contract and he wants more money upfront. If the team is agreeable, they could give him a large signing structure the deal like this:

$12M signing bonus
$4M base salary in year one
$7M base salary in year two
$7M base salary in year three
$10M base salary in year four

Now, the accounting gets fun.

The signing bonus is just what is says: a bonus for signing the contract. The moment the player signs the deal, the team owes him that money (whereas the base salary, even for the first year, is still contingent on Star Receiver being on the team each week).

This gives Star Receiver security right off the bat so

that no matter what happens, he has $12M. This is a pretty big incentive for a player.

At the end of the first year, all 17 installments of the $4M base salary would have also been paid out and Star Receiver would have made $16M.

If the salary cap accounted for all of that money right away in the year it was paid, it would be difficult on teams. At the same time, for obvious reasons, players want that money right away. This is where players and owners used accountants to figure out an agreeable solution in the CBA.

While salary for each year counts against the cap in the year it's paid, the signing bonus, though it is *paid* right away, incurs a cap hit that gets spread out across all the years of the deal (to a maximum of five).

So, in the scenario about, the amounts that would be *paid* each year are different than the amounts that count against the cap each year.

Amounts paid each year:
$16M base salary in year one ($4M salary plus $12M bonus)
$7M base salary in year two
$7M base salary in year three
$10M base salary in year four

Cap hit each year (base salary plus $3M prorated signing bonus each year):
$7M base salary in year one

$10M base salary in year two
$10M base salary in year three
$13M base salary in year four

Simple enough, right?

Where things get tricky is when a team decides that a player isn't worth their salary any more and wants to cut the player.

Let's say Star Receiver gets lazy and his play drops off, so the team cuts him after two years.

Star Receiver has been paid $23M, but only $17M of that has been counted against the cap in those two years. This would be an accounting loophole that teams could exploit by paying large bonuses, spreading out the cap hit, then cutting the player before the cap hit ever accrues.

That's where accelerations kick in.

If a player is cut, all of the remaining prorated signing bonus that is spread over future years immediately accelerates into the current year's salary cap.

So if the team cuts Star Receiver after year two, their year two salary cap hit would jump from $10M to $16M (because the $3M hits that would have been realized in years three and four would immediately get added to the ledger for year two).

Ouch.

This is where June 1st becomes an important date.

June 1st is the day each year where the fiscal year turns over from a salary cap accounting perspective.

So, in the example above, if the team waited until June

1st to cut Star Receiver, that cap year would already be in year three. The base salary wouldn't be due to the player (since they weren't on the team for the games), but the cap hit for the prorated signing bonus would spread out a little more.

The cap hit would still be $10M for year two. Then, on June 1st, when year three starts, there would be a $6M cap hit, representing the $3M per year that was supposed to come off the cap in years three and four. This is a way for teams to balance their cap from year to year.

Regardless if teams make the cut before or after June 1st, the bonus money that was paid needs to be accounted for in the salary cap - it's just a matter of which year they take the hit.

This is why it's a bit of a fallacy to say that a team "created" cap space.

Teams *cannot* "create" cap space, they can only move it around. Squeezing a balloon does not add more air into it.

Because of the nature of the accounting associated with signing bonuses, teams use them in a variety of ways to manage their cap from year to year. If they need to cut a player, they may do it before June 1st if they have room under the cap and just want to bite the bullet. Or, if they are tight in the budget, they may wait until after June 1st.

Players don't want to sit around waiting until June 1st to get cut (when they could be out looking for a new team), so the CBA allows teams to cut a player earlier and simply "designate" them as a post-June 1st cut.

In this case, a team may draft a new young receiver in April, realize they don't need Star Receiver anymore, and want to cut him right away. If they don't have enough cap space to absorb the signing bonus acceleration, they can cut Star Receiver right away and designate him as a post-June 1st cut, allowing them to shift the accelerated cap hit into the upcoming year and gain added flexibility in managing their cap.

Another way teams can leverage signing bonuses to manage their cap is by converting base (which is accrued in the same year it is paid) salary to a signing bonus (which is paid right away, but has a cap hit that can spread out of many years).

Let's say Fast Cornerback is starting year three of a five-year deal and a player is due a base salary of $9M. If the cap for the team is tight, they could convert that $9M base salary into a signing bonus. This works just like they renegotiated the exact same contract with two minor changes:

1. Fast Cornerback doesn't get his base salary doled out to him in prorated checks over 17 weeks, he gets it all the second he signs the deal.
2. The $9M no longer all counts against the current years cap, it gets spread out over the length of the deal (just like a regular signing bonus). In this case, there would be a $3M cap charge assessed in each of the remaining years (which would be in addition to any other currently existing base salaries or prorated signing bonuses).

This trick is a short-term fix, which creates pressure in future caps and is often done with only a portion of the base salary (so the player still has some incentive to play well that year). A team is still paying the same amount of cash to Star Receiver in the same year, but they are accounting for the money against the cap in future years.

This can, however, make future years difficult.

I repeat: there is no way to "create" cap space, you can only move it around.

If you convert a lot of players' salaries to signing bonuses, your cap will free up a lot in the short term, but once all those deferred cap hits accrue... oh boy.

INCENTIVES AND OTHER BONUSES

Base salaries and signing bonuses are usually negotiated based on what a player has done in the past and what they hope they will do in the future, but what if a team wants to compensate a player based on what they actually do accomplish in the future?

Well, in that case, there's a bunch of different bonus types teams can use.

Roster bonus

This is a bonus just for being on the roster at a certain point. It's usually a way for teams to limit their risk.

If a team isn't sure how long Aging Guard will continue to perform at a high level, they may structure some of the compensation as a $1M bonus to Aging Guard if he's still on the roster for the first game of the season two years from now.

If a team isn't sure if Injured Safety will be able to return to form, they could limit their risk with a roster bonus due in Week 5, so if he doesn't return to form, the team can cut him without paying the bonus.

These bonuses are similar to base salary in that they're payments scheduled for the future, but they are a single lump sum payment, not spread out over 17 games. This usually forces teams to make a decision on a player at a given point in time.

Workout bonus

Teams can use workout bonuses as a bit of a carrot to make sure a player is regularly performing their body maintenance.

If a team is concerned about Young Linebacker's work ethic, they may install a bonus for him if he attends all the off-season workouts. If a team wants to make sure Injured Cornerback is rehabbing at the team facility, they could add a form of workout bonus.

Similarly, players can be given bonuses on more concrete things, like weight. If a team thinks Big Nose Tackle (who regularly gets up to 350 pounds in the off-season) needs to be at 325 to be in optimal playing condition, they may have a bonus that pays him $20k for each week he weighs in at 325 or lower.

Statistical milestone and recognition bonuses

These bonuses are based on a player achieving a specific statistical level (like a $1M bonus if the quarterback throws at least 30 touchdowns) or gaining recognition in the awards season (a $2M bonus if the defensive lineman is voted to the First Team All-Pro squad).

Stat-based bonuses are a great way to pay for production, but they can also become a point of contention between players and coaches, especially late in the season.

If Star Receiver needs 1,000 yards to qualify for a $500k bonus, he might start to get antsy halfway through the season if he doesn't feel like his number is being called often enough. If Young Running Back gets a $1M bonus for getting 10 rushing touchdowns, he may get upset if a role player gets the ball on goal line for short yardage runs.

In cases like this, players may make passive-aggressive remarks or get outright confrontational with coaches. Fans sometimes underestimate the impact that locker room struggles like these can have on a team.

Statistical bonuses should be used with caution.

Recognition-based awards tend to be a bit safer. Players often get bonuses for making the Pro Bowl, being named to the All-Pro team or winning Offensive or Defensive Player of the Year awards.

Those honors are more dependent on how a player performs and less on how a coach calls the games.

All of these bonus targets are set prior to the season, but the results won't be known until after the season.

So how are they accounted for in the salary cap?

This is where the accountants that worked on the CBA had to put some clear rules in place.

When the year starts, these incentive-based bonuses are classified as likely to be earned (LBTE) or not likely to be earned (NLTBE).

LTBE are bonuses based on milestones or honors that were achieved the year before. So if Tall Tight End needs 500 yards to earn a $750k bonus, and he had 650 yards the year before, it would be considered "likely" that he would earn that bonus for accounting purposes.

If Short Tight End needs 500 yards to earn a $750k bonus, but he only had 400 yards the year before, his bonus would be considered "not likely" to be earned (NLTBE).

For the purposes of the cap, LTBE incentives are counted against the cap for the upcoming season and NLTBE incentives are not. In the scenario above, Tall Tight End's yardage bonus would count against the cap, but Short Tight End's bonus would not. Even though the bonuses are identical, their performance the year before determines if they are considered likely or not.

Then, when the dust settles on the season and the final stats are tallied, the accountants sort things out.

If a LTBE bonus is earned during the season, or a NLTBE bonus is not earned during the season, the cap charges don't change.

However, if a LTBE bonus is not earned during the season, the team would get a cap credit for the following year's salary cap. Alternatively, if a NLTBE incentive was earned, the team would have to account for that bonus on the following year's salary cap.

This ensures that the piper is always paid - there are

no ways to avoid cap hits on any money that is paid to players (at least not legally).

Playoff bonuses

Players on teams that make the playoffs get additional bonuses as a simple reflection of their team's success (motivation generates competition, which makes the league more entertaining and therefore more profitable).

Following the 2019 season, every player on a wild card team earned a $28k bonus ($31k if their team had won their division), players on teams that made it to the Divisional round each got $31k, and teams that played in the conference championships got $56k per player. Super Bowl losers got $62k, while the winners each got $124k.

These bonuses come directly from the league as a part of a separate funding pool, so they do not count against a team's salary cap.

Performance-Based Pay

Remember when I said that the CBA is an agreement between players and owners (and a whole bunch of accountants)?

One of the primary goals of the players in this negotiation was to make sure they weren't underpaid (they weren't nearly as worried about being overpaid). Because rookies are given slotted contracts based on where they are drafted, it's very possible that rookies (especially those drafted in the later rounds) could outperform their first contract.

To address this concern, the owners agreed to the concept of a performance-based pay pool, which was later expanded to also include veterans.

If a player exceeds certain playing thresholds, and has a salary that is lower than most players that play that much, he receives a bonus from the performance-based pay pool.

The pool is funded out of the same shared revenue pool that the salary cap and playoff bonuses come from. Like the playoff bonuses, these bonuses do not count against an individual team's salary cap.

The Top 51 rule

During the regular season, team rosters are limited to 53 players.

In the off-season, rosters expand to 90 players, allowing teams to work out extra players and generate competition in training camp.

This would put a lot of pressure on the salary cap if there weren't any exceptions.

Since the bottom of the roster often fluctuates in the off-season and accountants don't want to do a lot of unnecessary paperwork, the CBA dictates that only the 51 largest cap hits on the roster "count" in the off-season. It's a simple, elegant solution known as the Top 51 Rule.

Once final roster cuts are due, and the team has 53 players, all of those contracts and their various bonus structures need to fit under the cap.

. . .

Further Reading

This is just the beginning of understanding the salary cap for the purposes of understanding free agency at a high level. For a full understanding of the fascinating details, please read my companion book: A Fan's Guide To The NFL Salary Cap.

4

FREE AGENT TYPES AND TAGS

Not all free agents are created equal. Remember, this is a union shop, so seniority rules.

A player becomes a free agent after their contract expires, but tenure still matters. The number of years a player accrues determines if they are an exclusive rights free agent, restricted free agent, or unrestricted free agent.

Exclusive Rights Free Agents

If a player only has accrued one or two seasons of service when their contract is up, they are considered an Exclusive Rights Free Agent (ERFA). An ERFA isn't really much of a free agent at all. If their team offers them a qualifying offer (one year at the league minimum), the player either has to sign the contract or sit out.

It's a cruel world for the newbies in the union.

. . .

Restricted Free Agents

If a player has accrued three seasons when their contract is up, he becomes a Restricted Free Agent (RFA). An RFA has a little more bargaining power. RFAs are free to negotiate with other teams once free agency begins, but prior to the start of free agency, their original team has the opportunity to extend a qualifying tender offer.

There are four different tiers to the tenders - first-round tender, second-round tender, original-round tender, and the right-of-first-refusal tender - and each tier carries a different minimum qualifying offer amount (and those amounts change every year).

The first-round tender is the most expensive. If a team offers a player a contract at the first-year tender (or 110% of their previous salary, whichever is greater), other teams can still attempt to sign the player to a better deal once free agency officially begins. The original team, however, has the right to match the deal. If they don't, the new team has to give the original team a first-round pick as compensation.

The second-round tender works the same, except the tender amount is a little lower and the compensation (as you may have guessed) is a second-round pick. The original-round tender is an even lower amount and the compensation would be a draft pick in the round that the player was originally drafted in. So if a player was originally drafted in the sixth round, the new team would owe the original team a sixth round pick if they signed them. If the player was originally an undrafted free agent, there would be no compensation.

The right-of-first-refusal tender is a little different.

Teams have to offer a contract of a certain threshold (with no qualifier on the 110% rule that applies to the other three tenders) to maintain the ability to match any other the player signs. If they don't choose to match the offer, the team does not receive any compensation.

Unrestricted Free Agents

After four accrued seasons, players graduate to Unrestricted Free Agent (UFA) status.

When a UFA's contract is up, he can negotiate with any team he wants and sign with whoever he pleases. This is the level of free agency that players aspire to - total freedom!

There aren't a lot of rules around this, it's pretty simple, except...

What about those poor owners who have to watch their favorite star players just walk away with no compensation?

Remember, the CBA is an agreement between players and owners (and accountants) and the owners had some things that they wanted out of this whole arrangement, too.

When league owners agreed to let players pursue contracts with any team once their deal was up, they wanted some conditions for their core stars, so they wouldn't be left high and dry.

This is where the tags come into play for UFA's.

Franchise Tag

When an unrestricted player's contract is up, if their team thinks they're a premier player and a must-have guy that they can't live without, they can designate him as a franchise player by using this tag.

There's two versions of the franchise tag: the exclusive rights franchise tag and the non-exclusive rights franchise tag (very creative names that were most likely developed by the accountants).

With the exclusive rights franchise tag, the player is bound to the team for one year, but they get paid either the average of the top 5 players at their position or (if they are already making more than that) 120% of their previous salary.

This is a balance between a team telling a player that he has to stay with them and the player making sure he gets paid a boatload of cash in exchange for his limited freedom.

After that year, the player will become a free agent again... unless the team decides to apply the franchise tag *again*.

If a team franchises a player for a second consecutive year, they have to pay him 120% of his previous salary. And if a team wants to use a franchise tag on a player for a *third* consecutive year, they have to pay him 144% of their previous salary.

Yup, it gets expensive in a hurry - if you're going to force a player to stay somewhere he doesn't want to be, you're gonna pay through the teeth to do it. Plus, all franchise contracts are fully guaranteed.

That last point is important because if a team uses the tag out of bad faith (i.e., they intend to rescind it later), the player can call their bluff by signing the contract and locking themselves into a huge payday.

With the exclusive rights franchise tag, players don't really have any options. They can either sign the one-year franchise deal (and get paid a ton), negotiate a longer-term contract instead (which is sometimes the end goal of applying the tag), or just not play.

If a team uses the non-exclusive version of the franchise tag, the player is free to negotiate with other teams, but if a team signs him to a contract offer, the team that tagged the player has the right to match the deal and keep them. If they don't match the deal, the new team has to give the old team two first-round draft picks as compensation for the player.

It's hard enough to sign a superstar player to a mega-deal and fit it under the cap, but when you have to give up two first round picks on top of it, the investment becomes even harder to swallow (not to mention the fact that you go through all that work and the other team might match your offer anyway and make all that effort a big waste of time). This is why many teams don't even bother trying to sign another team's franchise players.

Getting a franchise tag usually means the player stays with their team or is traded.

Transition Tag

If a player is really good, but maybe not quite valuable enough to warrant the use of a franchise tag, teams can use a transition tag.

The process is similar to the franchise tag, but with a

transition tag, the salary is an average of the top 10 salaries at the player's position instead of the top 5.

There is no "exclusive" version of this tag, either, so any transition player is free to negotiate with other teams. If another team signs the player to a contract offer, their current team will have the right to match the offer. If the team declines to match the offer, they receive no compensation.

The transition tag is often used when a team and player are really far apart on salary expectations. Applying the tag allows both parties to see what the market for the player actually is.

Teams can only use one tag each season. If a team has more than one huge superstar, can't-live-without player, they better have a plan.

The tags are wonderful tools for maintaining balance, allowing teams to get a return on their investments in a player, and ensuring that no player gets stuck in a situation where they are grossly underpaid (at least not for too long).

———

Having a basic understanding of how contracts and the salary cap work is just the beginning.

Putting that knowledge into action is where GMs make their money. How do you balance all those contracts? How do you decide which players are worth bringing in and which aren't?

In the next section, we'll look at some landmark free agency cases to see what worked and what didn't.

PART II

CASE STUDIES

5
_____

REGGIE WHITE - HOW FREE AGENCY
WAS BORN

A ny delve into free agency stories has to start with Reggie White because, as far as the NFL is concerned, he is where free agency started.

Up until 1992, there was a very limited form of free agency system called Plan B, where teams could "protect" 37 players (out of the 47 man roster) from free agency, essentially keeping the core of their team intact, allowing for a long-term power imbalance among teams, and proverbially holding players hostage.

This was the crux of the class-action antitrust lawsuit that Reggie White led in White v. NFL, where White, on behalf of 280 players with expiring contracts, sued the NFL for the right to choose their next team.

Despite NFL attorney Frank Rothman's assertion that allowing free agency "would be the destruction of the National Football League," the courts ruled in favor of the players and free agency as we know it today was born.

Players and owners didn't agree on things (which is

pretty common in lawsuits), so Federal Judge David Doty basically told the teams and players that they had to agree on a system or he would put something in place himself.

That spurned action and the first CBA was drafted.

Reggie White, one of the greatest players in NFL history, was now a free agent.

Suitors lined up for the man who made the All-Pro team the previous seven years in a row. White had 124 sacks in 121 games over 8 seasons with the Eagles (after two years in the USFL, where he got 23.5 sacks). Every team wanted a player like that and thanks to the recent ruling, he was free and had his choice of destination.

An ordained minister, White claimed he would go wherever God told him to go. This prompted Packers head coach Mike Holmgren to leave a message on his answering machine that said "Reggie, this is God - go to Green Bay."

He did.

He cited a game he'd played against the Packers the previous season when he sacked their young quarterback Brett Favre, hitting him hard enough to dislocate his shoulder. Favre stayed in the game and that toughness was a draw for White.

The Packers, knowing he was a relationship-focused man, sold small town Green Bay as a college atmosphere and close-knit community where he could have an impact beyond the football field.

Undoubtedly, a contract that made him the highest paid defensive player of all time helped, too.

In White's six years with the Packers, he became the

franchise's all-time sacks leader, made the first or second All-Pro team every year, won Defensive Player of the Year, was named a member of the All-Decade team for the 90s, the 75th and 100th Anniversary All-Time Teams, and went to the Hall of Fame. The Packers retired his number, put his name on their ring of fame, and named a street after him.

All in all, he did ok for the Packers.

The team added aging star Sean Jones to be his defensive line bookend, along with former Defensive Rookie of the Year DT Santana Dotson and Gilbert Brown, building one of the most dominant defensive lines the league has seen in recent memory (all signed as free agents). The defense allowed 19 TDs (the 3rd fewest ever allowed in a 16 game season up until that point) and were the top scoring defense in the NFL.

They won the Super Bowl in 1996, in large part behind the strength of their defense.

Reggie White was everything every team could dream for when signing a free agent.

LESSONS LEARNED

The lesson right from the start is that if one of the best players in the history of the league becomes a free agent in his prime, signing him might be a good idea.

What many fans translate this to is "pay whatever it takes to get a great player because it guarantees a Super Bowl win!"

This is where things get dicey.

People that use Reggie White as an example of

anything are missing critical parts of the history behind this landmark signing.

The truth is this type of value is unrepeatable - even in the unlikely case that a better player comes along.

Reggie White's case was unique for many reasons. Not only was free agency a new concept that owners and GMs really didn't really understand, there was also a one-time stipulation afforded to White as a part of the initial settlement.

Today, a player of White's caliber would undoubtedly be slapped with the exclusive franchise tag, meaning other teams wouldn't even be able to try to negotiate with him.

Even if he only got the non-exclusive rights franchise tag, a team would have to give up two first-round draft picks as compensation if they could sign him. This normally deters other teams from trying to sign a player of that caliber.

In White's case, as one of the five named plaintiffs in the class action suit, he was given a special quid pro quo exception: not only could he not be slapped with the exclusive franchise tag, if a team signed him, they would not have to give up two first round picks (the Eagles were instead awarded a bonus compensatory pick at the end of the first round of the 1994 draft as compensation).

This means that the Packers got a franchise-level player, which should require giving up two first round picks in compensation, without giving up anything.

This had never happened before and will never happen again. This is why Reggie White is an exception to the free agency rules.

Simply put, the lesson learned here is to never compare a free agency signing to Reggie White. It's unlikely any free agent will play at the level White played at, teams now have a way to block a player like that from even negotiating with other teams, and it's impossible to get a player of that magnitude without giving up picks in return through the tagging process.

Packers used their next two first round picks on Aaron Taylor and Craig Newsome - both starters on their Super Bowl winning team of 1996. Without the draft pick exemption (a one-time deal for White and the other four named members of the landmark class action), it's possible the Packers don't sign White or, if they do, they miss out on those two pieces of their championship roster and never win a Super Bowl with Reggie White.

It's impossible to know how things would have played out, but we do know this: there will never be another free agent situation as rare as Reggie White's.

Key Lesson: Use Reggie White's case as a basis for understanding the history of free agency and how it can be used for building a team, but do not use it as an example when considering future signings, because the context and terms have changed drastically.

6

BRYCE PAUP - CATCH A PEAKING PLAYER

L et's turn the tables a little and look at a pass rusher that did phenomenal *after* leaving the Packers.

Bryce Paup was an unheralded prospect out of Northern Iowa. He had the build at 6'5 250, but never stood out in college and had a poor combine workout. The Packers drafted him in the 6th round of the 1990 draft.

He was a part time starter his first couple of years, but proved to be a late-bloomer, eventually earning a full-time starting position and averaging about 8 sacks per season.

He signed with the Bills for $7.6M on a three-year deal. Packers GM Ron Wolf thought the price tag was too high, given that Paup's success came while offenses focused on blocking Reggie White and Sean Jones. Wolf would later say it was a mistake on his part and Paup would claim it was a huge motivator for him.

In his three-year stint in Buffalo, a highly motivated

Paup went to the Pro Bowl every year, won Defensive Player of the Year, and averaged double-digit sacks every season.

Pretty successful.

After Paup's three-year deal was up with the Bills, he signed with the Jaguars for a five-year, $22M deal. Over the first two years of the deal, he played in 31 games, totalling a meager 7.5 sacks. The Jaguars needed their outside linebackers to drop back in coverage frequently, which was not Paup's strength and impacted his numbers significantly.

The Jaguars cut him with three years left on his five-year deal, flushing cash and incurring cap penalties on the prorated signing bonus.

Then, at age 32, Paup signed with the Vikings. Never able to crack the starting lineup, he got 2 sacks and 7 tackles in spot duty and his career ended after one year in Minnesota.

LESSONS LEARNED

Scheme played a role in Paup's productivity at each of his stops. In Green Bay, he was a 4-3 outside linebacker, used almost exclusively as a situational pass rusher. In Buffalo, Paup played a 3-4 edge rusher role, which suited his abilities even more, and his production exploded.

The Jaguars went the opposite route. Paup was still physically capable, but his pass rushing skills were never on display when he was dropping back into coverage in Jacksonville's scheme. He was just not a good defensive fit there.

Paup showed his work ethic and ability on the Packers. The Bills did their scouting homework and signed him to put him in a system that would play to his strengths and maximize his impact. More accurately stated, the Bills were looking for players that would fit the new defense that Wade Phillips was installing and they nailed it with Paup.

The Jaguars did the opposite.

Jacksonville fell into the trap of trying to assemble a group of good players and then just throwing them together. The result was a complete misuse of a very expensive player's skill set. The Jaguars signed a fierce pass-rushing edge linebacker and put him in a defense that needed linebackers to play in space and cover.

His productivity dropped (predictably) and the team eventually cut him, wasting time, talent, and money.

Key lesson: Don't sign a great player if the things that make him great won't be used in your scheme.

7

ALBERT HAYNESWORTH - MONETARY MOTIVATION

T he Jaguars paid a price for a mis-valuing a player, but it was not nearly as big of a price as the Redskins did with Albert Haynesworth

At 6'6" 315, with a solid Pro Day, Haynesworth didn't even need to participate in the scouting combine to convince teams of his potential - the Titans selected him at number 15 overall.

In his first five years, he was a solid player. He played out his $8.3M contract and was looking for a big deal. The best he could get was a two-year $12.8M extension from the Titans. It wasn't peanuts, but it wasn't the big-money deal he was seeking.

With age creeping up, he knew he only had one chance left for a big contract. He put in the work and took his game to another level. After never having more than 3 sacks in a season, he registered 6 and then 8.5 while putting up some of his best years in tackles and setting new career marks for passes defended, forced fumbles, and fumble recoveries.

After never even making a Pro Bowl in his first five years, he was voted First Team All-Pro in back-to-back seasons.

He hit free agency playing the best football of his career and playing like one of the best defensive linemen in the game.

But football performance was only one aspect of the Haynesworth equation that teams had to consider.

In his second training camp, he got into a scuffle and ended up kicking teammate Justin Hartwig while he was down and had to be held back by teammates.

In a 2006 game against the Cowboys, Haynesworth ripped off Dallas center Andre Gurode's helmet and kicked him in the head with his cleat, opening a wound that required 30 stitches to close and earning him the longest suspension in NFL history for an on-field incident

In 2007, right after signing his two-year extension with the Titans, he was fined for his actions in the very first game of the season.

Now the question was: would anyone pay big bucks to such a huge character risk, especially one who only seemed to turn it on when he knew he needed a big contract?

As the answer almost always is: you're darn right.

The Redskins had hovered around .500 the previous two seasons and needed a boost to their defense. They re-signed cornerback DeAngelo Hall to a monster deal, but needed help on the defensive line.

So they offered Haynesworth a $100M contract.

The Buccaneers reportedly offered him a $120M contract, but the Redskins deal had more guarantees (an

NFL-record $41M guaranteed). Such a guarantee meant that Haynesworth would get an absolutely ridiculous amount of money, even if his play fell off the map and he was terrible.

Which he was.

Because of course he was.

Immediately upon arrival in Washington, he was a problem, criticizing the coaching staff for playing him at nose tackle (the position they paid him $100M to play). His sack totals cut in half and his tackles - and effectiveness - dropped considerably.

The Redskins fell from an 8-8 squad on the edge of the playoffs to a 4-12 unit, despite the talent upgrades. The defense, which signed Haynesworth and spent a top 15 pick on pass rusher Brian Orakpo, gave up 40 more points than they had the previous season.

Haynesworth's problems in year two started before the season even began. He wouldn't participate in off-season workouts, and when he did eventually report, he was so out of shape that he couldn't even pass the team's basic fitness tests to participate in practice.

His sack total fell to 2.5 and his tackles dropped to a career-low 16, in part because the team suspended him for his behavior.

The following training camp, he was traded to the Patriots for a fifth round pick. They cut him mid-season after he clashed with an assistant. The Buccaneers picked him up, played him seven games, then cut him, ending his career.

The Onion ran a headline in 2010 stating "Report:

Albert Haynesworth Just A Mound Of Ice Cream And Hot Dogs."

You know you messed up when The Onions jumps in.

LESSONS LEARNED

Oh boy, is there a lot to dig into here!

For starters, it always looks fishy when a guy is a solid player for his whole career, then, when his contract comes up, he (literally) turns into an All-Pro.

As if that wasn't enough of a clue that he's in it for the money, he took a smaller contract (from a state with higher income taxes) because it had more guaranteed money.

Players are human and some are just motivated by money. When those guys get the money, they often put less effort into their play. Albert Haynesworth seemed to be one of those guys. If turning it on only when he was coming up for a contract didn't send the message that he was only doing it for the money, then taking a smaller contract with more guarantees should have.

When guys are motivated by money, the results when they get money are often predictable.

There were also the behavioral red flags.

After the fights with his own teammates and the fines and suspensions, Washington should have known better.

And they did.

And they still took the chance.

And they failed.

It's the nature of the NFL to overlook a mountain of

red flags if a guy has talent. Teams are so desperate for talent that they refuse to learn this lesson.

This is not some kind of revisionist history, where we look back and say "oh, they should have known" when no one had any idea. All throughout the free agent process, people commented about the dangers and risks associated with giving Albert Haynesworth a Brink's truck.

The Redskins accepted those risks. They hoped they would be the team to make this troubled player work out or at least keep him contained for a little bit.

They weren't.

Now they're a case study in bad free agency moves.

Key Lesson: Don't give a ton of money to a player who only performs in contract years and has a ton of behavioral issues.

8

ANDRE RISON - PLAYING WITH FIRE

Andre Rison is another troubled player that hit free agency, but he worked out... at least for a little bit.

Drafted in the first round by the Colts, he ran into team offices to demand what was wrong with his first paycheck... because he didn't know what taxes were.

This should make it unsurprising that he would go bankrupt after making over $20M in salary and endorsements. This is also a sad indicator about how unprepared and immature some of these guys are for what comes with being in the NFL. They lack perspective and awareness and aren't always emotionally equipped to handle the strains and pressure of the game and what comes with it.

The red flags of maturity coupled with behavioral issues for doing things like getting arrested for going 72 miles per hour *over the limit* (not just 72, but 72 *over* - he was doing 128 in a 55) was enough to convince the Colts to include Rison as part of trade package with the Falcons to move up in the draft, despite a very promising rookie season.

Andre Rison, troubled as he was, had a productive five-year stretch with the Falcons, averaging over 1,100 yards and 11 touchdowns per year while making four Pro-Bowl teams and earning a First Team All-Pro honor.

However, he was also involved in numerous off-the-field incidents during that time. He was charged with aggravated assault, discharging a firearm, and a host of other charges in his tenure with the Falcons.

The most famous incident came in 1994, a year after leading the NFL in touchdown receptions. He was in a troubled relationship and his girlfriend burned down his mansion, bringing to light a lot of the personal issues that were easier to keep quiet in the days before social media.

His production dipped the following year, he was suspended by the team, and after his contract was up, the Falcons opted not to re-sign him.

The Browns, who went to the playoffs at 11-5 the year before, were looking to bolster their receiving corps. Despite the red flags and long history of issues, they made Rison the highest-paid wide receiver ever, with a five-year $17M contract that included a $5M signing bonus.

On the field, Rison's style and habit for ad-libbing his routes didn't mesh well with timing-based quarterback Vinny Testaverde and off the field, his attitude didn't play well with fans. After being booed most of the season, Rison jabbed back at Cleveland Browns fans (who were upset that the team announced they were moving to Baltimore) with an expletive-laced rant ending in "Baltimore, here we come."

Rison never made it to Baltimore, though.

When new coach Ted Marchibroda came on board, one of his first moves was to cut the troubled receiver only one year after signing a five-year mega-deal.

The Jaguars tried their hand at signing Rison next, figuring maybe they could be the team to tame him, but no-nonsense head coach Tom Coughlin was having none of Rison's nonsense and cut him mid-season.

What kind of team would take a chance on him after all that?

The answer, as is usually the case, was: a desperate one.

The Packers had lost Sterling Sharpe to a career-ending neck injury in 1994. Then Robert Brooks stepped up to become a top five wide receiver in 1995. Unfortunately, in 1996, he blew out his knee. Antonio Freeman stepped up and became the man, then broke his forearm in the middle of a Super Bowl run.

The Packers needed another wide receiver.

Desperately.

By this time, they were about the only team in the league willing to take a flier on him. It was already late in the year - all they needed was for Rison to stay out of trouble for a couple months. A locker room full of positive veteran leaders like Reggie White and Sean Jones were counted on to keep him in check just long enough to win the Super Bowl.

They did.

After claiming Rison off waivers for $350k over 5 games, Rison became the solid supporting receiver the team needed and in the Super Bowl, on the Packers first pass play, he blew past coverage for a 54-yard touchdown.

Rison was a savior of sorts for the Packers 1996 Super Bowl team.

Then he was gone.

He had stayed out of trouble for a couple months. The Packers got what they needed and didn't press their luck.

He went to the Chiefs for a few years and eked out a Pro Bowl before a couple mediocre years, then got one more chance with the Raiders, but couldn't even crack the starting lineup by that point.

Throughout his career, he was a troubled, but very talented, player that couldn't hang on in one place very long because of his off-the-field issues. The rare combination of talent and trouble ended up making him the only player in league history to have scored a touchdown for seven different teams.

A dubious distinction.

LESSONS LEARNED

Whenever anyone brings up Andre Rison as a free agent, they talk about his time with the Packers.

Here's the thing, though: the Packers didn't even sign him as a free agent.

The Browns signed him as a free agent and threw away an enormous signing bonus to cut him after one year.

The Jaguars signed him as a free agent, but couldn't even handle him for that long.

The Chiefs signed him as a free agent and squeezed a

solid season out of him, but by then he was pretty much washed up.

The Raiders signed him as a free agent, but his skills were already so diminished that he was off to the CFL after one year.

The Packers claimed him as a waiver pickup, risking about 0.3% of what the Redskins signed Albert Haynesworth for (plus, since he wasn't a free agent, he didn't impact compensatory picks).

The risk was very little.

The reward was pretty high.

He was a key role player for the Packers's Super Bowl run, but only because he was a tiny financial risk, joining a team that already had the top offense in the league, and had a locker room full of leaders like Reggie White and Sean Jones to keep him in line.

Even with that, he barely lasted a couple months.

The Packers signed him to be a short-term role player, while the Browns, Jaguars, and Chiefs were depending on him to be the centerpiece of their offense.

Depending so heavily on a free agent who's never played with your team - and has a history of serious off-field issues - is a dangerous proposition.

In most of Rison's stops, he had problems meshing with the team. With the Falcons, his propensity to miss meetings was overlooked and changing routes didn't matter as much in the wide-open Red Gun offense.

Then the Browns made the mistake of trying to bring that play style into an offense that didn't support it, in addition to bringing that personality into a locker room that couldn't handle it.

The Jaguars made the same mistake. Mark Brunell threw 18 interceptions in 11 games with Rison. Much was made of the fact that Rison would change his routes, leading to interceptions. Rison left and Brunell settled down, finishing the season with 4 straight games of 0 interceptions.

A quick look back at the coaches shows what a mistake his signings were, too. The Jaguars were just being silly if they thought they could bring a wild card like Rison into a locker room run by Tom Coughlin. Ted Marchibroda had already proven that.

Key lesson: High-risk players pay the most dividends when they are brought in on low-risk deals, but teams need to do their homework on character issues because staying out of trouble for a couple months doesn't mean a player's problems are a thing of the past.

9

DESMOND HOWARD - ROUND PEG

Now let's look at one of Rison's Super Bowl teammates, Desmond Howard.

Howard was a Heisman winner and a talent so great that the Redskins traded a first-round pick to move up *two spots* and ensure they got him. His underwhelming rookie year ended with 3 catches for 20 yards despite playing all 16 games. After three years with the team, he was left unprotected for the expansion draft and was selected by the Jaguars.

In his lone season in Jacksonville, he only had 26 catches and 1 touchdown, cementing his status as a draft bust.

The next year, he signed with the Packers on a one-year "prove it" deal for $300k with no signing bonus.

He had a terrible preseason as a receiver and wasn't going to make the team until he returned a punt 77 yards for a touchdown, prompting the Packers to keep him as a full-time returner.

He couldn't even break 100 yards receiving on the season, despite being on a team decimated by injuries at receiver. However, he flashed his rare athleticism as a returner and led the league in punt returns, punt return yards, punt return average, and punt return touchdowns as well as being a dangerous kickoff returner.

In the playoffs, he racked up nearly 500 return yards and two touchdowns in three games. In the Super Bowl, he broke the return yardage record, scored on a 99 yard kickoff return, and won MVP.

The next year, he signed a four-year, $6M contract with the Raiders, who expected him to contribute as a receiver as well as a returner. Through two years, he caught only six balls and was cut.

He finished his career bouncing between the Lions and Packers, but still only managed 12 catches in his final three seasons.

LESSONS LEARNED

Let's overlook the obvious gaffe in draft evaluation and the terrible value in using a first-round pick to trade up two spots and just focus on the lessons we can learn about free agency.

Looking back, it's pretty easy to see the difference between what the Packers succeeded at and what the Raiders failed at in regard to Desmond Howard.

The Packers signed him for next to nothing and then used him in the role he excelled in - returning.

The Raiders then signed him to a big deal to be a wide receiver, ignoring his abysmal production as a receiver on the Redskins, Jaguars, and Packers.

Giving money to a one-year wonder is one thing, but

giving money to a guy who was a one-year wonder at a different position than the one you want him to play is just silly... but when it's another position that he has already failed at repeatedly with no signs of improvement... well then it's one of the worst ideas ever in free agency.

Key lesson: If a payer succeeds at one thing and fails at another, don't sign him to do the thing he failed at.

DREW BREES - AN INJURED FREE AGENT

Quarterback is the most important position in the game and the most difficult position to play. Teams do everything they can to get one that's even halfway decent and once they have one, they don't let them go.

It's extremely rare to have a chance at a good quarterback in free agency, but it happened with the most prolific quarterback in NFL history.

Drew Brees had a record-breaking college career and was a Heisman finalist twice, but teams were still leery of how good he could be in the NFL because of his 6'0" frame.

The Chargers, who had 5'10" Doug Flutie as a starter, weren't scared off by his height and took him in the second round of the 2001 draft..

He became the starter in his second year and after a couple inconsistent seasons, the Chargers drafted Philip

Rivers in the first round of the 2004 NFL draft to be his replacement.

Brees responded with his best season as a pro, earning a Pro Bowl berth in 2004 and winning the Comeback Player of the Year award. He played the 2005 season under the franchise tag and in the last game of the year, suffered a brutal injury, dislocating his throwing shoulder while fully tearing his labrum and significantly damaging his rotator cuff.

The injury clouded his future in free agency.

Could he recover from such an injury? He'd tore his ACL in high school, did this mean his undersized frame just wasn't cut out for football?

The Chargers already had his replacement on the team. They weren't desperate, so they offered him a short, incentive-laden deal. Most teams were wary of signing a quarterback to a significant contract while he was recovering from such a huge injury to his throwing shoulder.

The Dolphins seemed poised to land him, but in the final reviews of his medical condition, team doctors recommended against signing him and they signed Daunte Culpepper instead.

That left the Saints with the only reasonable offer, with a middle-of the pack average salary of $10M per year.

They signed him to a six-year contract, and the rest is history. His first year with the Saints, he led the league in yards and was a First Team All-Pro.

He went on to win a Super Bowl (and Super Bowl MVP) en route to setting the all-time NFL records for passing completions, yards, and touchdowns.

He is one of the best free agent signings of all time.

. . .

LESSONS LEARNED

It's tough to sort through the lessons here because no team did anything that looks stupid, even in hindsight.

From the Chargers perspective, it's hard to fault them for drafting Philip Rivers, a highly rated prospect, after Brees failed to impress in his first three seasons.

While his next two years were more impressive, it's hard to fault them for moving on to their young prospect after Brees suffered such a significant injury to his throwing shoulder.

The Chargers made the safe move.

The Dolphins trusted their doctors. The lesson for them might be simply to get better doctors. Dr. James Andrews performed the surgery and said he nailed it, but I still haven't seen a doctor finish operating on an NFL player and say "boy, I really botched that - this dude's career is done."

The Dolphins also made the safe move.

For the Dolphins, and 30 other teams, it became a game of odds. The odds just weren't high that an under-sized quarterback, coming of a devastating injury to his throwing shoulder, would break all the major passing records in the league.

The Saints took a more optimistic approach. They looked back to see that after his ACL tear in high school, he rehabbed hard, and came back to lead his team to a state title and an undefeated season. They saw that his last two years showed a lot of growth and improvement after his first three.

Then, they took a leap of faith that he could show the same resilience from injury that he did in high school and continue the growth trajectory he had seen more recently.

However, their leap of faith came with a reasonable contract offer, not an inflated, desperate one.

The big red flags the Saints had to consider with Brees were size and injury. Since he'd already proved he could be effective in the NFL at his size, the biggest remaining question was how he would recover from his injury.

One of the key factors that separates him from those other stories is the red flag he didn't have: attitude.

The Saints took a moderate financial risk at a critical position for an injured player with a reputation for being a great teammate and locker room presence.

The worst-case scenario was his shoulder hadn't recovered enough for him to return to Pro Bowl form.

This was not a situation that was likely to end with his demeanor and behavior tearing a locker room apart, causing a bunch of controversy, and ending with him getting cut for his attitude and incurring a big cap penalty.

The only question the Saints had to wonder about was if his shoulder would heal enough for him to return to form.

They were right. It paid off big time.

Here's where fans can get frustrated. They see a story like this - a huge exception to a clear rule - and say "take a chance - look what happened with Drew Brees!"

But look what happened to guys like Jim McMahon, Chad Pennington, Andrew Luck, Cam Newton, and Aaron Rodgers after their throwing shoulders were damaged - they didn't bounce back.

Brees is an outlier.

Key Lesson: Players who don't have an attitude problem can be worth a calculated injury risk (especially at a critical position) with a reasonable contract because the worst-case scenario isn't all that bad.

11

BROCK OSWEILER - DOUBLE WHAMMY

Injuries aside, quarterback is still a tough position to scout and a position teams are desperate to fill.

Brock Osweiler was a top quarterback prospect coming out of college. The Broncos selected him in the first round of the 2012 draft as the future starter to aging starter Peyton Manning.

Osweiler sat on the bench for his first three years behind the future Hall of Famer. Then, in 2015, with Manning hurt, Osweiler was thrust into a starting role. In seven starts, he led the team to a 5-2 record with solid, though unspectacular play, leading a run-based attack that gained nearly 1,000 yards in seven games.

His play kept the team in contention and helped them earn a crucial bye week in the playoffs so Peyton Manning could return fully rested and lead the Broncos to a Super Bowl win over the Panthers.

In the offseason, his poise down the stretch garnered

the interest of the Texans, who had won their division on the strength of a tough defense and good skill position players, despite a revolving door of starting quarterbacks including Brian Hoyer, Ryan Mallett, TJ Yates, and Brandon Weeden (even BJ Daniels got some playing time).

The Texans felt like they were just a quarterback away from a title and felt Osweiler could be their answer. They signed him to a gaudy four-year $72M contract.

He was benched before he made it through one season.

Tom Savage took over, but got hurt, forcing Osweiler back into the starting role for the playoffs, where he threw three interceptions in a season-ending loss to the Patriots.

This is where things get really funny.

In the offseason, the Texans traded Osweiler, a second-round pick, and a sixth-round pick to the Browns... for a fourth-round pick.

You read that right.

The Texans traded Osweiler away - and gave up draft capital - just to get him off the team. The Browns took on Osweiler's ridiculously over-market contract just so they could get some extra draft picks.

The Browns paid out his remaining $15M of salary guarantees, then cut him before the season even started.

Interestingly enough, he re-signed with the Broncos (for far less money) after their backup quarterback got hurt. Osweiler ended up starting four games and losing them all. The Dolphins picked him up as a backup the following year, he didn't fare well, and retired the following season.

· · ·

LESSONS LEARNED

The Texans did what so many teams do: whatever it takes to get a quarterback.

In my book *A Fan's Guide To The NFL Draft: Strategies, Tactics, and Case Studies on Building a Professional Football Team*, I talk about the vicious cycle that teams go through to find a quarterback and why GMs will do anything - no matter how stupid - to get a chance at one.

In this case, the Texans proved the point.

They had a solid running game, a dangerous receiving core, and a championship-quality defense.

All they needed was a quarterback.

They didn't need a great quarterback, though, they just needed one that was good enough to not lose games for them.

They judged Osweiler on less than half a season's work, which resulted in barely average production, and made a gigantic contract offer out of desperation.

In their rush, they overlooked the fact that Osweiler was leading the most dominant ground game in the league during that stretch of the season. They saw the team's success and attributed way too much of it to the quarterback. Osweiler got the keys to a championship team and kept the engine running.

The Texans supporting cast, as good as it was, wasn't at the same level as the Broncos. They misjudged how good Osweiler was and they misjudged how good their team was. They got excited and grossly overpaid.

They blew their chance for a special season and paid dearly in draft picks and social embarrassment to get rid of their mistake.

Key lesson: don't make moves out of desperation.

12

MATT FLYNN - A MODEST, HEDGED BET

Teams find themselves in situations like the Texans were in (a good team that just needs a quarterback to lead it) all the time, but they don't all approach it with the same blind desperation.

The 2011 Seahawks had a strong running game led by Marshawn Lynch, a strong receiving core, and a tough defense featuring the Legion of Boom.

They did not, however, have a quarterback.

The 2012 free agent market was light on quarterbacks. Peyton Manning was coming off a neck injury and headed to Denver. The next biggest name on the market was Matt Flynn.

Flynn was a career backup with the Packers, who raised some eyebrows with his performance in the last game of 2011. While the Packers rested their starters for the playoffs, Flynn stepped in to throw for 480 yards and 6 touchdowns against the playoff-bound Lions.

The Seahawks signed him to a modest three-year,

$20.5M contract - a reasonable deal for a largely unknown commodity.

A month later, the Seahawks hedged their bets and drafted Russell Wilson in the third round. Wilson won the starting job over Matt Flynn, tied the rookie record for touchdown passes, and went on to make seven Pro Bowls and win a Super Bowl.

After one year on the team, Flynn was traded to the Raiders for draft picks.

LESSONS LEARNED

If the Seahawks had made a desperate move in free agency like the Texans did when they signed Brock Osweiler to a $72M deal, they may have felt handcuffed into going all-in with door number one.

But they didn't act out of desperation. They acted more like the Saints and took a calculated risk. They also hedged their bets with a draft pick, giving them two opportunities to find a starting quarterback, neither of whom would destroy their salary cap if they didn't work out.

Very few people outside of Seattle remember that the Seahawks signed Flynn shortly before drafting Wilson, and even fewer hold it against them. This was one of the best examples of a failed high-profile free agent that didn't really hurt the team.

It's not very often that a team signs a free agent to be their starting quarterback, fails, and then moves on without any long-term repercussions.

The Seahawks did it because they didn't mortgage their future. Instead, they hedged their bets.

Key lesson: If you make reasonable moves and take calculated risks instead of overly aggressive splashes, you'll be ok if it doesn't work out. Also, hedge your bets at important positions.

13

PRIEST HOLMES - A SMALL BET PAYS OFF

Priest Holmes had a nondescript college career, serving as a backing up Ricky Williams. He joined the Ravens as an undrafted free agent and continued his backup role behind guys like Errict Rhett and Jay Graham.

In his second year, he finally got a chance to start and rushed for 173 yards against division rival Bengals. He followed that up with an inconsistent 6 game stretch before rushing for 227 yards in his second game against the Bengals.

Despite rushing for 400 yards in two games against the Bengals, he barely rushed for 600 yards in his other 14 games. Over the next two seasons, he was outshined by Errict Rhett and then Jamal Lewis.

As a free agent in 2001, the Chiefs - who had a committee backfield - signed him to a modest 5-year $11.7M contract to be a part-time player.

They liked what they saw in his running style and thought they could be a good fit in their offense.

They could not have imagined he would fit as well as he did.

In his first year with the Chiefs, he led the league with 1,555 yards rushing. In the following two years, he combined for over 3,000 yards rushing and led the NFL in rushing touchdowns with 21 in 2001, then 27 in 2002. He was a First Team All-Pro in each of his first three seasons with the Chiefs.

In 2004, he was having another phenomenal year and was on pace to set career highs in yards and touchdowns, before a knee injury ended his season.

The following season, he looked like he was making a strong comeback until he suffered a spinal injury that effectively ended his career.

LESSONS LEARNED

This is another case of player fit, but also a textbook example of how mid-tier free agents can flourish in the right situation..

Holmes's college career was cut short by injury, and he was always a backup with the Ravens. Guys like Bam Morris and Errict Rhett had better reputations and got the playing time ahead of him in the pros. Holmes flashed potential when he filled in as a starter, but also had some games that were downright stinkers.

The Chiefs weren't desperate for a starter with a specific skill set to fill a defined role. They just wanted a player to add a role player to their running back group. This flexible approach was a big factor in their success.

They made a modest investment on a high-potential player, rather than an enormous investment on a high potential player (as is often the case in free agency). When Holmes produced in their system, the Chiefs adjusted their offensive approach to compliment him and eventually designed their entire offense around him.

If Holmes had the breakout year he had in his first year with the Chiefs while he was still with the Ravens, he would have been a sizzling hot free agent prospect and landed an enormous deal. Whichever team won the bidding war may have seen similar production (if their offense allowed it), but they would have realized far less value, since they would have paid a much bigger price.

Priest Holmes joining the Chiefs was the perfect storm of free agency: an underutilized talent in a poor scheme fit that will fit his new team better that signed an affordable deal with a team that wasn't desperate.

Key lesson: Don't focus your free agent search solely on the big-name guys who have already produced; look for role players who show the potential to be more productive in a new scheme.

14

ADALIUS THOMAS - THE PATRIOTS
BIG MISS

A dalius Thomas was a little-known sixth round pick for the Ravens in 2000 who worked hard to become a special teams leader and carve out a niche role on defense.

When Peter Boulware was injured in 2004, the Ravens promoted Adalius Thomas to a starter at outside line-backer and he responded with a surprising 8-sack season.

The Ravens were so impressed with this play that they released Boulware prior to the 2005 season, making Thomas the full-time starter.. Over the next two years, he racked up 20 sacks, scored 4 defensive touchdowns, and earned a First Team All-Pro spot.

Like Albert Haynesworth, he peaked just in time for free agency.

Unlike Albert Haynesworth, he didn't have a history of behavioral problems or give any reason to believe his productivity would drop.

The Patriots - notoriously shrewd in free agency -

79

signed Thomas to a five-year $35M deal in 2007, making him the most expensive free agent in Patriots history to that point.

Thomas grew into a pass rushing specialist with the Ravens as an outside linebacker. Naturally, he assumed that if the Patriots were paying him so much, they would want him to do the same thing.

The Patriots had other plans.

In New England, Thomas was played at inside linebacker. Instead of rushing around the edge to attack the quarterback, he was fighting through pulling guards and blocking fullbacks to take down running backs. Instead of being a featured star of the defense, he was rotating with veterans Junior Seau and Tedy Bruschi.

Thomas's production dipped immediately. His sack total of 6.5 was the lowest since he had become a full-time starter. The following two years saw his sack production drop even further, first to 5 then to 3 and his tackle production fell off a cliff after his first year, dropping from 79 to 33 to 34.

Frustrated with his role, Thomas lashed out publicly. He was deactivated by head coach Bill Belichick, who had a reputation for not responding kindly to players who behave that way. Thomas grew even more vocal, saying that motivation was for kindergarteners.

The Patriots tried to trade him, but couldn't find a willing partner, so they simply cut him with two years left on his deal, eating nearly $5M of prorated signing bonus.

He never played again.

. . .

LESSONS LEARNED

In this case, the Patriots strayed from what they normally did well. They have a history of finding cheap veteran role players to be good short-term patches. This time, they made a splash for a big name All Pro.

When searching for role-players to use as a patch, the Patriots are looking for a specific skill set to use in a specific position and the match usually works out very well. When recruiting an All-Pro, the conversation changes - those guys aren't expected to fill a small role, they're expected to do everything.

In this case, that message may not have been clearly communicated.

Adalius Thomas's comments made it pretty clear that he was not expecting to fill the role that the Patriots had in mind. Thomas thought he was coming to New England to rush the passer just like he did in Baltimore. The Patriots clearly had different responsibilities in mind for him.

If you're going to spend more on a free agent than you ever have in the history of your franchise, you should probably have a good long talk with that player and clearly lay out expectations of what responsibilities he will have in the scheme.

If they nod their head and say "yeah" while staring slack-jawed at the big number on the contract, you might need to tap their shoulder and make sure you have their attention.

Key lesson: Communications are key to expectation-setting - don't assume you are on the page without confirming.

15

DWAYNE BOWE - A GAME OF INCHES

D wayne Bowe was a top wide receiver prospect coming out of college and the Chiefs took him in the first round of the 2007 draft.

In his first six years with the team, he averaged almost 1,000 yards per season, made a Pro Bowl, and even led the league in touchdowns one year.

After that level of production, the team wanted to keep him when his contract expired. Even though he was nearing 30 years old (a key age plateau at the position), the Chiefs gave him a 5-year $55M contract.

Over the next two years, he only averaged 700 yards per season, failing to even score a single touchdown in 2014. The Chiefs realized they made a mistake and cut him, accelerating a $9M cap hit just to get him off the team.

It seemed his career would be over, no team would be desperate enough to sign an aging receiver who had just been cut because his production had fallen off a cliff.

Or would they...

Just one month before the Chiefs cut Bowe, the NFL had announced that Josh Gordon, the Browns top receiver, had been suspended for the entire 2014 season.

When Bowe hit the open market, the Browns wasted no time pursuing him and decided it would be a good idea to sign the 31-year-old receiver, coming off a year where he was held scoreless all season, to a 2-year, $13M deal with $9M in guarantees.

How did that work out?

Bowe couldn't even crack the starting lineup.

He barely even managed to earn any playing time. He was only active for 7 games, in which he had 5 catches for 53 yards and no TDs.

The Browns cut him after his first season with the team.

Bowe never played again.

LESSONS LEARNED

The Chiefs took a bit of a chance when they gave Bowe a contract extension at age 30 and hoped he would continue his same level of production.

It's not an uncommon mistake. Teams value the continuity that comes with keeping players in their system and it can be hard to predict exactly when age will catch up to them. They clearly miscalculated and made the mistake of paying a player based on past performance (which is also not an uncommon mistake in free agency) rather than future potential.

The Browns were downright foolish.

They weren't taking a risk that a player would continue to perform in their system. They panicked and acted out of desperation when their top receiver was suspended and gave a tone of money to an aging player who clearly was past his prime.

There weren't a lot of big-name receivers available in that free agent class, so they overpaid the biggest name out there and ended up cutting him after one season.

His contract had $9M in guarantees.

He only managed 53 yards.

That means that Bowe made $169,881... per yard.

That's 56,603 per foot.

The Browns paid Dwayne Bowe over $4,716 per inch!

That's a bad deal.

Scratch that - that's a *terrible* deal.

Key lesson: Don't sign aging players experiencing production drop offs to large contracts because you're desperate.

16

DARRELLE REVIS - THE SERIAL FREE AGENT

Darrelle Revis was the epitome of shutdown corner, the best defensive back of his generation.

He was also a unique case study in free agency. There has never been a player so forward about his intentions to want to be the highest-paid player at his position and taking so many actions to get more money through free agency.

He left college as a junior and was such an impressive prospect that the Jets traded up to get him in the first round of the 2007 draft.

He was not as anxious to join the Jets as the Jets were to get him, though.

In the days before rookies were given slotted deals, Revis held out for a large contract, missing the first 21 days of training camp and only getting action in one preseason game, so that he could maximize the value of his first contract.

Despite missing so much practice, he started every game for the Jets as a rookie and earned a spot on the All-Rookie team.

Over the next four years, he made four consecutive Pro Bowls and was a First Team All-Pro three times, earning a reputation for not giving up any catches and garnering the nickname "Revis Island" for his ability to shut down a team's top receiver in one-on-one man coverage.

Four years into his six year rookie contract (when he was scheduled to earn $1M), he held out of camp for a bigger contract again. His holdout was successful again, and he got a four-year $46M contract (technically a seven-year deal with a void clause after four years) reporting just a week before the first game of the season.

After two years in his new seven-year deal (which was supposed to be good for at least four years), Revis started to hint that he wanted another new contract. After year three, when Revis talked more about wanting a new deal, the Jets grew tired of the constant holdouts and traded him to the Buccaneers for a first-round pick and a fourth-round pick.

The Buccaneers gave Revis an enormous six-year $96M contract, making him the highest-paid defensive back in league history.

At least the Buccaneers were smart enough to not include a lot of guaranteed money upfront given his history. That turned out to be a smart move, because after one season, even though he played well enough to be voted to the Pro Bowl, the Buccaneers cut him because his salary was just too big.

This would become a theme for Revis.

Next, he signed a two-year $32M deal with the Patriots, got paid, won a Super Bowl, and was cut after one year because of his salary.

Then he signed with the Jets again on a five-year $70M deal. Two years into that contract, his play had dropped off at the age of 31, and he was too expensive to keep at his enormous salary.

The Chiefs signed him to a two-year deal, but ended up releasing after six games and he announced his official retirement that offseason.

LESSONS LEARNED

Darrelle Revis was a unique story. As soon as he was drafted, he made it known that he intended to get paid. Every team, every contract, every year, he lobbied for more money, holding out regularly, despite being under contract.

On the flip side, he was a dominant player, racking up Pro Bowl and All-Pro honors like few others. The Patriots signed him to get another Super Bowl, and he matched up on number one receivers all year and only allowed a total of one catch in the AFC Championship Game and Super Bowl combined.

You have to be that good to get away with what he got away with.

Revis never stayed anywhere long-term. He was a mercenary, a player for hire who was always looking for the situation that would benefit him the most financially.

He signed six contracts with four different teams and

never played out any of them. He earned over $118M throughout his career, maximizing his earning power in a way few, if any, other players ever have.

He is the far end of the pendulum. In many ways, he's the purest businessman the game has ever seen. He may be the future of how players behave. Teams would be wise to keep this case in mind when negotiating with players.

Key lesson: Don't believe that a player will honor his contract and never trust Darrelle Revis if he says he won't hold out.

17

THE 2011 EAGLES - THE DREAM TEAM

So what happens when free agent players band together to try to form a super-team like in the NBA?

The 2010 Eagles looked like a team on the rise, winning the NFC East and qualifying for the playoffs for the third year in a row on the strength of the highest-scoring offense in the conference led by a renaissance year from Michael Vick.

In the off-season, the Eagles turned to free agency to improve their defense and started by signing cornerback Nnamdi Asomugha, a four-time All-Pro and the prize of the 2011 free agent class.

They also signed Cullen Jenkins (the best defensive lineman available), defensive end Jason Babin (who had just earned his first Pro Bowl berth), and safety Jarrad Page (an apparent upgrade from their incumbent starter).

They also improved their offense by signing Pro bowl running back and former #2 overall pick Ronnie Brown and bolstered their offensive line by signing guard Evan Mathis and tackle Ryan Harris.

Quarterback Vince Young, a former #3 overall draft pick, who had been the starting quarterback for the Titans the year before, even signed on to be the backup because he wanted to be a part of what everyone was calling "The Dream Team" - a squad so improved through free agent signings that they basically *had* to win the Super Bowl.

Or so they thought.

That's the funny thing about football.

Remember earlier when we talked about how football isn't like baseball or basketball? Remember when we talked about a football team needing to be a cohesive unit, not just a collection of players?

This might be the best example of that idea in the history of the NFL.

The Dream Team, a Super Bowl favorite for most pundits, started the season 1-4. They stumbled to 4-8 before barely managing to salvage a .500 season.

They missed the playoffs for the first time in four years and only the third time in the last twelve years.

It was not a good dream.

LESSONS LEARNED

Football is a complex game with a lot of moving parts and a complex web of matchups.

Baseball and basketball are about one-on-one matchups, football is about how eleven players can move together in concert.

It's not enough to sign a bunch of talented players and throw them on the field together. Players need familiarity to play off one another and they need to be put into a scheme that maximizes their unique skill sets.

It's this delicate balance that makes football so challenging and entertaining.

Looking back at the case studies of individual players, we see this idea on a small scale. The Eagles 2011 Dream Team is how it plays out on a large scale.

Any fan that thinks their team just needs to sign a free agent or two to be guaranteed a Super Bowl needs to remember the Dream Team.

Key lesson: Free agency cannot be used to buy a championship in football, the game is too complex.

18

BROADER HISTORY

E valuating players in football is one of the most difficult jobs in sports.

Rookies can take three or four years to reach their potential (longer in some cases), and it usually takes a similar window to see how a free agent will work out, too.

A free agent usually needs to play out his contract before you can judge if the move was a success or not.

To analyze how big-name free agents have fared over the years, we went back and looked at the top 10 free agents (as rated by the NFL) that signed with new teams for the 2014, 2015, and 2016 seasons.

Of those 30 players, the most highly sought-after free agents in the league over three years, only three players actually played out their contract.

Of those three, two of them were one-year deals.

Neither of the players on one-year deals were re-signed by the team after the year was up.

Think about that.

Megastars become available in free agency, teams make giant plays to get them, investing huge amounts of money and planning the futures of their teams around them... then end up cutting them before the contract is up and taking huge cap hits for accelerated bonus amounts.

Let's look at the top names from those three years, the number one free agent gem from each class and see how they fared:

- 2016: Malik Jackson signs with the Jaguars for six years and $90M. He lasted three years before getting cut.
- 2015: Ndamukong Suh signs with the Dolphins for six years and $114.4M (the largest contract for a defender in NFL history). He made it three years before getting cut.
- 2014: Jairus Byrd signs with the Saints for six years and $54M. He also lasted three years before getting cut.

The biggest name in free agency for each of those years signed a mega-deal and only played for half the contract.

Not only is that disappointing from a team and talent perspective, it also incurs a big cap hit when the bonus money is accelerated. The team loses a big player and loses cap space they could have used to replace the player.

Free agency is no sure thing.

To quote 6-time NFL Executive of the Year Bill Polian again: "Free agency is almost always a bad proposition."

19

EXERCISE

I f this all sounds interesting, and you want to get an even deeper understanding of how free agency works in the NFL, I'd encourage you to do this (seemingly) simple exercise each year during the first week of free agency.

As big-name players start signing big-money deals, look at which ones you think are good deals and which ones are good fits.

Mark down which players you think will have good seasons with their new teams, which players you think will actually play out their full contract, and which teams you think will show significant improvement based on the players they picked up. Make any other predictions you have about how the moves will pan out, too.

Save the list (physical or digital) and pull it out next year between the Super Bowl and the start of free agency (that time of year gets boring, anyway) and see how you did. What did you learn? Equipped with that new knowledge, make your notes for the new free agent class and go back to both lists the following years.

I do this exercise every year and never cease to be amazed by how totally wrong I am.

Free agency is not easy and there are never guarantees.

If you're interested in football enough to read this book, I think you get a lot of entertainment from this exercise.

Enjoy.

20

WRAP UP

Overall, big free agency contracts usually don't end well.

Teams see a player perform well on another team and want to bring them into their team.

When things work out well, the results are spectacular. Priest Holmes was one of the best values ever in free agency and launched the Chiefs offense from a middling unit to a group that led the NFL in scoring by a wide margin in back-to-back years.

But for every Priest Holmes, there are far more cases like Adalius Thomas and Brock Osweiler where big splashes crash and burn, leaving nothing but regret and cap hits in their wake.

The best values in free agency rarely come from the biggest contracts.

The siren song is loud, though. GMs and fans alike are lured by the appeal of adding a star player to their team, even though history shows the moves are rarely worth it.

They all share the same hope: maybe this one will be one of the good ones.

Maybe it will.

I hope you've enjoyed this look into what makes free agency so compelling and dramatic, and I hope you've gained a better understanding of the process.

Most of all, I hope this book helps you appreciate how difficult free agency is, and enjoy it more as a result.

If you'd like to see more of my free agent coverage, feel free to follow me on Twitter at @PackersForTheWn or check out my website at PackersForTheWin.com.

THANK YOU

Thank you for reading!

I truly hoped you enjoyed delving deeper into NFL Free Agency strategy and history.

If you enjoyed this book, would you please consider leaving a five-star review? This link will take you to the page:

PackersForTheWin.com/ReviewFreeAgency

Reviews are the lifeblood of any book. Your review can help others find this book, in addition supporting me.

Thank you so much,

-Bruce

ABOUT THE AUTHOR

Bruce Irons is a fan of football who has watched, played, coached, studied, and thoroughly enjoyed the sport for decades.

You can read more of his analysis at:
  PackersForTheWin.com

You can also follow him on Twitter:
  @BruceIronsNFL

BOOKS BY BRUCE IRONS

A Fan's Guide To Understanding The NFL Draft: Strategies, Tactics, And Case Studies For Building A Professional Football Team

A Fan's Guide To NFL Free Agency Hits And Misses: Case Studies And Lessons From Landmark Signings Throughout History

A Fan's Guide To Understanding The NFL Salary Cap: How The NFL Salary Cap Works And Why It Matters